I Wonder Why

Baby Animals

Hannah Wilson and Nicki Palin

KINGFISHER

First published 2008 by Kingfisher
an imprint of Macmillan Children's Books
a division of Macmillan Publishers Limited
The Macmillan Building, 4 Crinan Street, London N1 9XW
Basingstoke and Oxford
Associated companies throughout the world
www.panmacmillan.com

Consultant: David Burnie

ISBN 978-0-7534-1683-9

1 3 5 7 9 8 6 4 2
1TR/0408/LFG/UNTD/140MA/C

A CIP catalogue record for this book is available from the British Library.

Printed in China

Contents

Baby animals

Thousands of baby animals
are born every day. Feathery
chicks and scaly lizards hatch
from eggs. On hot, grassy
plains, furry lion cubs and
big baby elephants
are born.

baby deer

mother
elephant

1. Why is a baby deer spotty?

2. Where do baby animals live?

3. What does a baby elephant look like?

antlers

baby deer with stag (father)

tusk

1. A baby deer has spots to help it hide in the grass. Its father has horns on his head, called antlers.

2. Baby animals live in many different places. Some babies live in water or on ice. Other babies live in hot jungles.

3. A baby elephant looks like its mother, but it is much smaller and has no tusks.

Where some baby animals live

Ducklings live in water.

Some baby seals live on ice.

Baby monkeys live in hot jungles.

5

Furry babies

A furry baby animal grows inside its mother's body. When it is born, the baby drinks its mother's milk. The milk helps the young animal become strong and healthy.

mother koala up a tree

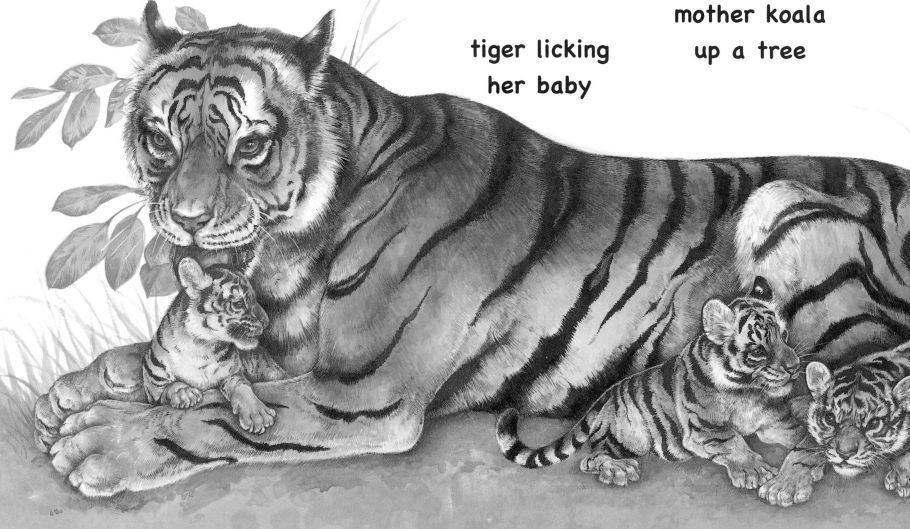

tiger licking her baby

1. How does a koala carry her baby?

2. What do baby animals do all day?

3. Why does a tiger lick her baby?

koala baby on mother's back

cubs drinking mother's milk

1. A koala carries her baby on her back. The baby is too small to look after itself.

2. Baby animals eat and sleep. Young chimpanzees also like to play.

3. A tiger licks her baby to clean its fur. A baby tiger is called a cub.

Baby chimpanzees

eating

sleeping

playing

Feathery babies

Baby birds are fluffy, but when they get older, their feathers grow stronger. This helps some birds, such as owls, to fly and other birds, such as penguins, to swim under water.

Penguin chicks huddle together to keep warm.

penguin with egg on feet

8

1. What grows inside an egg?

2. What do baby birds eat?

3. Who looks after a baby emperor penguin?

penguin chick has hatched

1. A baby bird, called a chick, grows inside an egg. When the egg hatches, the chick comes out.

2. Most baby birds eat the food their parents bring to the nest. Some chicks eat fruit or insects. Owl chicks eat mice.

3. The male penguin rests the egg on his feet. When it hatches, he keeps the chick warm under his feathers.

Owl chicks feeding

hungry owl chicks

adult brings a mouse

chicks eat the mouse

9

Scaly babies

Most baby reptiles, such as crocodiles and turtles, hatch from an egg. Scaly babies are often fully formed and look like tiny adults. They can look after themselves straight away.

baby chameleon

crocodile

10

1. How does a baby
chameleon catch
its food?

2. Where are baby
turtles born?

3. What does a mother
crocodile carry in
her mouth?

chameleon
catching a fly

1. The baby chameleon shoots out its long, sticky tongue to catch a fly.

2. Baby turtles hatch from eggs, buried on a sandy beach. They crawl down to the ocean to swim away.

3. A mother crocodile carries her babies inside her mouth to keep them safe.

crocodile babies swimming

Baby turtles being born

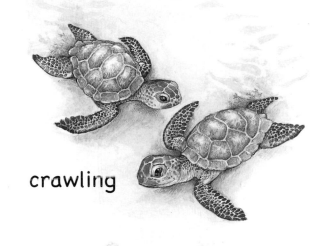

hatching from eggs

crawling

swimming

11

Water babies

All kinds of babies live
in seas, ponds and rivers.
Some water babies, such
as fish, can breathe under
water. Whales, dolphins and
hippopotamuses must swim
to the surface to breathe.

baby hippopotamus
swimming

1. Where is a baby hippopotamus born?

2. When does a baby hippopotamus learn to swim?

3. How does a tadpole turn into a frog?

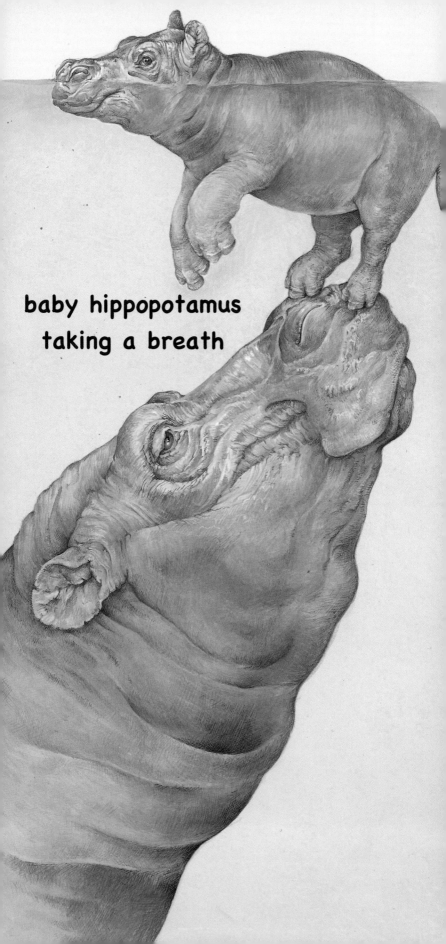

baby hippopotamus
taking a breath

1. A baby hippopotamus
   is born under water
   in a river or lake.

2. A baby hippopotamus
   must learn to swim straight
   away. Its mother nudges it
   up to the surface to breathe.

3. A tadpole grows back
   legs, then front legs.
   Finally, it loses its tail
   and becomes a frog.

How a tadpole becomes a frog

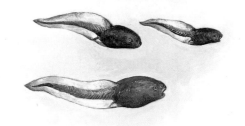

Tadpoles hatch from eggs.

Then they grow legs.

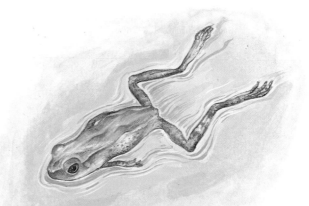

Each tadpole turns
into a frog.

13

Baby homes

Some animals build nests or dig burrows for their babies. Others set up home in caves or tree hollows. There are also some animals that keep their babies on their bodies.

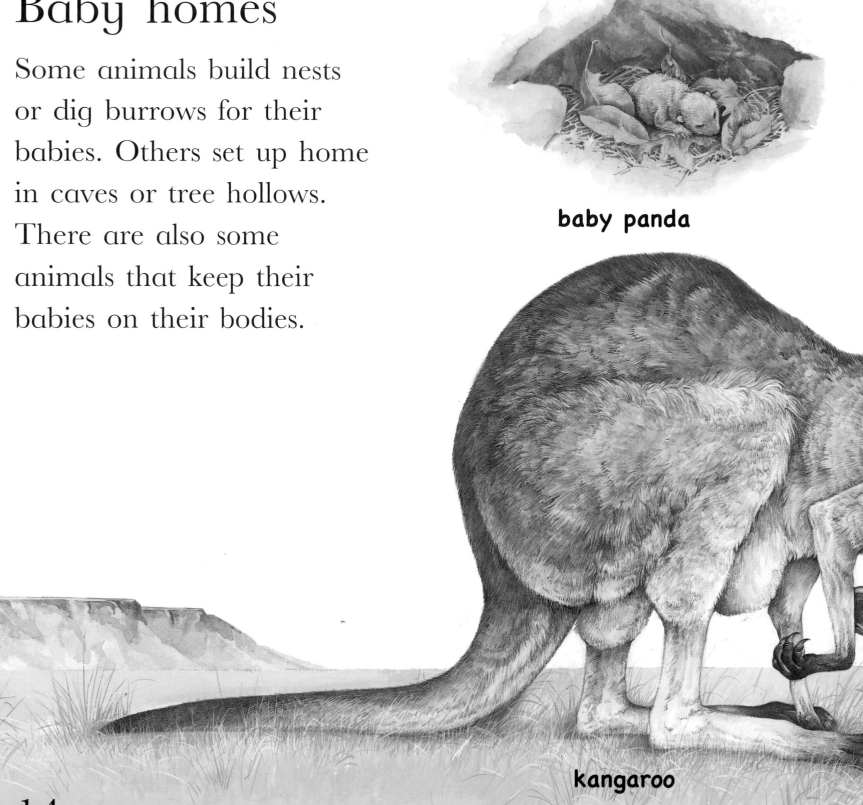

baby panda

kangaroo

14

1. Where does a
baby panda live?

2. Why do baby rabbits
live underground?

3. Who pops out
of a pouch?

older baby panda
eating bamboo

1. A baby panda lives in a cave. When it grows bigger, it can crawl outside to eat bamboo.

2. Baby rabbits live underground in a burrow. The burrow keeps them safe and warm.

3. A baby kangaroo is called a joey. It lives in its mother's pouch until it is about six months old.

joey in pouch

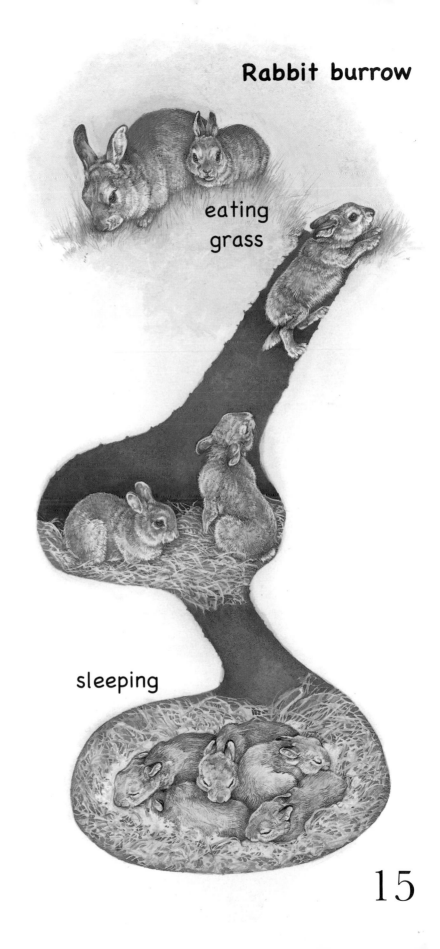

Rabbit burrow

eating grass

sleeping

Growing up

Many baby animals stay
with their mother or group
until they are big enough
to find food for themselves.
They leave when they can
walk, run or fly properly.

young bears
play-fighting

16

1. How do baby birds learn to fly?

2. When does a bear grow up?

3. Why do young bears fight each other?

one bear
wins the fight

1. Chicks grow long feathers and flap their wings to make them stronger. Then they try to fly from the nest.

2. A brown bear lives with its mother for three years. It becomes fully grown at ten years old.

3. Young bears play-fight because it makes them stronger, and it is fun!

Parrot chicks growing up

Chicks have soft feathers.

They then grow long feathers...

and learn to fly!

Index